THE WAY
GOD TEACHES

THE WAY GOD TEACHES:

Catechesis and the Divine Pedagogy

Joseph D. White, Ph.D.

OUR SUNDAY VISITOR PUBLISHING DIVISION
OUR SUNDAY VISITOR, INC.
HUNTINGTON, INDIANA 46750

Nihil Obstat
Msgr. Michael Heintz, Ph.D.
Censor Librorum

Imprimatur
✠ Kevin C. Rhoades
Bishop of Fort Wayne-South Bend
January 3, 2014

The *Nihil Obstat* and *Imprimatur* are official declarations that a book is free from doctrinal or moral error. It is not implied that those who have granted the *Nihil Obstat* and *Imprimatur* agree with the contents, opinions, or statements expressed.

ISBN: 978-1-61278-784-8 (Inv. No. X1590) (Hardcover)
ISBN: 978-1-61278-836-4 (Inv. No. X1643) (Paperback)
eISBN: 978-1-61278-359-8
LCCN: 2013957953

Cover design: Tyler Ottinger
Cover art: *Christ Enthroned: French Psalter Illumination*,
courtesy J. Paul Getty Trust
Interior design: Dianne Nelson

PRINTED IN THE UNITED STATES OF AMERICA

Table of Contents

Introduction

GOD SPEAKS TO US

"Wake up, Neo. The Matrix has you."

This is the opening line to the popular 1999 science fiction movie *The Matrix*, in which people's minds were imprisoned within an illusory world that they thought was real life. In some ways, there are parallels between the plot of *The Matrix* and the state of our contemporary society. Often the things valued by our society are fleeting "illusions," while it seems that we have forgotten what it means to truly be alive. What is the matrix in which we live? It's made up of many elements, including the following:

- *The tendency to value material goods more than people.* In the race to acquire material possessions, we lose sight of the most important things in life. So many around the world lack the basic necessities to survive, and yet others have so much more than they need. Jesus admonishes us, "Do not store up for yourselves treasures on earth, where moth and decay destroys, nor thieves break in and steal. But store up treasures in heaven, where neither moth nor decay destroys, nor thieves break in and steal" (Mt 6:19-20).

- *The busy-ness of the modern world that causes us to spend less time together and form fewer close relationships.* A recent study showed that adults in the United States have about half the number of close friends they did just ten years ago. This does not bode well for our future, since scientific studies in the mental health field tell us that social support serves as an important buffer against stress, depression, and other types of mental illness.

- *The cheapening of God's great gift of sexuality on the Internet, in movies, and on television.* In God's creation, human sexuality is a gift intended to bring married persons closer together and bring new life into the world. It is a visible sign of a complete gift of one's self to the other. And yet, in much of today's mainstream media, sex has become a recreational sport that turns people into commodities to be used up and discarded.

- *An almost overwhelming explosion of new electronic media,* which used correctly can bring people together, but used wrongly can distract us from genuine human relationships and time together.

- *A moral relativism that says there is no right or wrong — what matters is how you feel.* Cardinal Joseph Ratzinger, addressing the conclave that would elect him Pope Benedict XVI, stated, "We are moving toward a dictatorship of relativism which does not recognize anything as for certain and which has as its highest goal one's own ego and one's own desires."

- *A sound-bite culture that holds deep thinking and reflection at bay.* Intelligent discourse is rare in our society. The twenty-four-hour news cycle thrives on sensationalism and attention-grabbing sound bites. Real thinking and problem solving are often the casualties.

And yet, in the midst of this matrix, God speaks to us — teaching us, as he has since the beginning of Creation, how to be truly human, and what it means to "have life and have it more abundantly" (Jn 10:10). Are we listening? And are we helping others listen, too?

One key on how to pay better attention to God's message and hand it on to others may be in a study of *how* God teaches us. What is the pedagogy of God?

Chapter 1

WHAT IS THE DIVINE PEDAGOGY, AND WHY IS IT IMPORTANT?

"You have made us for yourself, O, Lord, and our hearts are restless until they rest in you." — Saint Augustine

God Reaches Toward Us

IN MICHELANGELO'S ICONIC IMAGE of the *Creation of Adam* on the ceiling of the Sistine Chapel, Adam is shown reclining lazily, with a disinterested expression of his face as he partially extends a finger toward God the Father. God, on the other hand, is fully leaning over toward Adam, his arm and hand extended completely in a dramatic and powerful gesture of mercy and humility. Why mercy and humility? Because God is GOD, and Adam is his creature. Yet it is God who reaches out. The Creator makes the first move to connect with the created.

We see a similar image as Jesus tells the story of the prodigal son (see Lk 15:11-32), who, although he has been given everything, chooses to leave his father and walk his own path. It is the story of all humanity. It is interesting to note that when the son finally comes to his senses, realizing that even the servants in his father's house live better than he is now living, the father sees him "while he was still a long way off" (v. 20). Why? Because even after all this time, *the father was looking for him.*

The Divine Pedagogy

God creates us out of love, and he creates us for love. We are made to be in relationship with him. And it is God who initiates that relationship. To us, he reveals the truth about himself and his Creation. We call the way God reveals his truth to us the *divine pedagogy*. The word "pedagogy" comes from the Greek word παιδαγωγέω, which means, "to lead the child." Likewise, God's own manner of leading us, his children, toward himself, is God's pedagogy.

"Concerning pedagogy," the *General Directory for Catechesis* (*GDC*) notes, "after a period in which excessive insistence on the value of method and techniques was promoted by some, sufficient attention is still not given to the demands and to the originality of that pedagogy which is proper to the faith. It remains easy to fall into a 'content-method dualism'" (30).

In other words, we tend to think of catechesis as being part content (what we teach) and part methodology (the methods we use). Over the past several decades in catechesis, we have seen the pendulum shift back and forth between emphasis on the content and attention to the process. We have sometimes even seen divisions between various camps that value one over another. Pitting content against process is destructive to catechetical ministry, for both are essential. If we are not handing on content that is true and complete, our catechesis is meaningless. Likewise, if we are not transmitting the Gospel in ways people can hear and understand our ministry becomes fruitless. Content and methodology are not opposite sides of the same continuum. Rather, they are both essential aspects of effective catechesis.

Pedagogy and methodology are not exactly one and the same, but rather pedagogy, with respect to catechesis, may be defined as "overarching principles of transmission, which govern the nature of catechesis precisely as the transmission of the faith" (Willey 2009). The word "pedagogy," then, can refer to the principles that govern both the selection of content *and* methods we use, more than the methods themselves. In this way, sound pedagogy can be seen as a bridge between content and methodology, a way to keep us out of the unhelpful content-method debate and refocus us on a catechesis that is both more intentional and freer from ideological agendas.

A Pedagogy for Catechesis

But what is the starting point for developing a pedagogy for the ministry of catechesis? The *General Directory for Catechesis* states, "Catechesis, as communication of divine Revelation, is radically inspired by the pedagogy of God, as displayed in Christ and in the Church" (143). We are called to hand on the truths of the faith not merely by doing our best according to human standards of theology and educational methodology, but rather by echoing God's own way of teaching us his truths. We must also respect that, even as we teach others, God remains active in the heart of the human person, bringing growth to the seeds of faith that are planted there. In other words, we echo God's own way of teaching, and then we also realize that the fruits that come from this are not from ourselves but from God.

By reflecting on the divine pedagogy, we can more fully inform our own thinking regarding formation in the faith, particularly with regard to content and methodology. Reflecting on the pedagogy of God can assist us in developing a way of catechizing that mirrors the divine pedagogy, keeping us focused on the content that is most important and helping us to select the best methods. For, as the *General Directory for Catechesis* asserts: "The Church, in transmitting the faith, does not have a particular method nor any single method. Rather, she discerns contemporary methods in the light of the pedagogy of God and uses with liberty 'everything that is true, everything that is noble, everything that is good and pure, everything that we love and honor and everything that can be thought virtuous or worthy of praise' (Phil 4:8)" (148).

The *GDC* asserts that it is the Church's mission to be "a visible and actual continuation of the pedagogy of the Father and of the Son" (141). Therefore, as Willey (2009) writes, "the Church as a whole incarnates the ongoing pedagogy of God, within which the catechist works, and provides the overall context for the animating activity of the Holy Spirit." The Church, in her discussion of the divine pedagogy, most particularly in *Dei Verbum* (*The Dogmatic Constitution on Divine Revelation*), the *Catechism of the Catholic Church*, and the *General Directory for Catechesis,* reflects upon several distinct but interrelated aspects of the pedagogy of God. This book will discuss five of these characteristics, with particular attention given to their application to contemporary catechesis in Catholic parishes and schools.

Questions for Reflection

- In what ways has God "reached out" to you?

- How have you accepted his invitation to relationship with him?

- What experiences do you have with the content versus methodology debate in catechesis?

Chapter 2

God's Pedagogy Is Directed Toward the Individual Human Person

"For man would not exist were he not created
by God's love and constantly preserved by it;
and he cannot live fully according to truth unless
he freely acknowledges that love and devotes
himself to his Creator." (Gaudium et Spes, 19)

These words from the Second Vatican Council's *Pastoral Constitution on the Church in the Modern World* speak to the truth that only God fully knows each of us, because he is our Creator. Because of his intimate knowledge of humanity in general, and each person in particular, God reaches out to us in a manner that fully reflects our human experience, our current situation, our ability, and our need.

Use of Human Experience

The field of cognitive psychology tells us that each person interprets the world in light of his or her own sets of assumptions and beliefs, largely based on his or her own experience. These sets of assumptions and beliefs are called *schemata*. Schemata assist individuals in incorporating and classifying new information (Neisser 1967).

Designed by God to receive his self-revelation, we are created such that our natural human experiences provide both opportunities to learn about God and bases for reflection on principles of faith. In this way, personal experience assists us in growing in knowledge of, and relationship with, our creator. Experiences that might be opportunities to grow in our faith include our relationships and interactions with others, events of daily life, and even difficult experiences in which we can see God at work, helping us to persevere and to overcome.

The *General Directory for Catechesis* states, "Experience, assumed by faith, becomes in a certain manner, a *locus* for the manifestation and realization of salvation" (152).

Adaptation to Culture and Situation

In revealing himself to humankind, God speaks in a language humans can understand. This is seen most clearly in the Incarnation of Jesus Christ, but additional examples include Jesus' teaching in parables, which were generally stories about ordinary persons and situations within the context of the culture and time. Adaptation to culture is seen in a striking way on the feast of Pentecost, in which the Holy Spirit enables the Gospel message to be heard by each person in his or her own language (see Acts 2:7-9). A further example is seen in the teaching of Saint Paul in the Areopagus, as he uses the Athenians' altar to an unknown god as a point of entry to preach the Gospel (Acts 17:22-31).

The *General Directory for Catechesis* states that God "assumes the character of the person, the individual and the community according to the conditions in which they are found" (139). Quoting Saint John Chrysostom, the Second Vatican Council speaks of the "marvelous 'condescension' of eternal wisdom ... 'that we may learn the gentle kindness of God, which words cannot express, and how far He has gone in adapting His language with thoughtful concern for our weak human nature.' For the words of God, expressed in human language, have been made like human discourse, just as the word of the eternal Father, when He took to Himself the flesh of human weakness, was in every way made like men" (*Dei Verbum*, 13).

God's adaptation of his Word to culture and situation has important implications not only for our catechesis of others, but also for our proper understanding of Scripture. This is discussed in *Dei Verbum*:

> Since God speaks in Sacred Scripture through men in human fashion, the interpreter of Sacred Scripture, in order to see clearly what God wanted to communicate to us, should carefully investigate what meaning the sacred writers really intended, and what God wanted to manifest by means of their words. (12)

We understand, then, that to properly interpret Scripture, we need to understand the cultural and situational context in which the human author is writing.

God Understands Our Limits, and Meets Our Needs

In our attempt to comprehend God, we are limited by our humanity. In this sense, one might argue that humanness itself is a disability with respect to the understanding of divine revelation. God, however, enters into solidarity with us, coming to us in the person of Jesus Christ, who accepted the limitations of humanity so that we might enter into relationship with him.

> God, wishing to speak to men as friends, manifests in a special way his pedagogy by adapting what he has to say by solicitous providence for our earthly condition. (*GDC*, 146)

In Scripture, we can observe several examples of God himself, as well as men and women who are led by God, accommodating not only for the special needs of the human condition in general but for various needs of particular individuals. For example, one might say that Saint Peter was impulsive. He was the first to jump out of the boat and walk on the water with Jesus, but he also lost focus, looking instead at the wind and waves, and sinking into the water. He impulsively cut off the ear of the soldier who came to arrest Jesus in the garden. He frequently spoke without thinking — at one point prompting Jesus to rebuke him with, "Get behind me, Satan!" (Mt 16:23). Yet Peter's gift of leadership, his boldness, and his ability to capture the attention of others, led Jesus to choose Peter as our first pope, and he remains one of the greatest saints in our history.

In Mark 2:1-12, we read the story of a person with physical disabilities whose friends want him to meet Jesus. Jesus is speaking in a house, and the crowds are so great that the men cannot even get their friend, whom they are carrying on a mat, in through the door. They take him to the roof, cut a hole in the roof, and lower him through.

In the Acts of the Apostles, Saint Phillip encounters an Ethiopian who is traveling through the desert. He is reading passages of prophecy related to the Suffering Servant, but lacking both the context of Jewish tradition and the knowledge of recent events concerning Jesus, he is unable to make sense of what he reads. Phillip offers to help, and after some study and discussion the Ethiopian responds to the Gospel message by being baptized (see 8:26-38).

God reaches out beyond the limits of human persons and finds a way to draw us to himself. In the Father's relationship with his people Israel, Christ's willingness to accept the limitations of becoming a human being, and the Holy Spirit's work in the apostles of Jesus, we can see God's desire to meet our particular needs and challenges, for his "power is made perfect in weakness" (2 Cor 12:9).

Questions for Reflection

- How has God taught you about himself through your life experiences, both in daily life and in major life events?

- How has God provided for your unique needs?

Chapter 3

A Catechesis Directed Toward the Individual Human Person

"Experience promotes the intelligibility of the Christian message. This corresponds well to the actions of Jesus. He used human experiences and situations to point to the eschatological and transcendent, as well as to show the attitude to be adopted before such realities. From this point of view, experience is a necessary medium for exploring and assimilating the truths that constitute the objective content of Revelation." (GDC, 152)

Personal Experience

CATECHESIS HAS THE POTENTIAL to both illuminate personal experience — to help us understand ourselves better — and also to be better understood in light of the experience of the individual. Because of this, we are admonished by the *General Directory for Catechesis* to make liberal use of human experience in our catechetical ministry, even when this makes our work more challenging: "Interpreting and illuminating experience with the data of faith is a constant task of catechetical pedagogy — even if with difficulty. It is a task that cannot be overlooked without falling into artificial juxtapositions or closed understandings of the truth. It is made possible, however, by a correct application of the correlation and interaction between profound human experiences and the revealed message" (153).

The *General Directory for Catechesis* describes a complex and multifaceted relationship between human experience and the Christian message, affirming that this relationship "is not a simple methodological question" (116). Rather, the *GDC* describes a catechesis in which the disciple is simultaneously engaging in learning the story and ways of Jesus while at the same time attending to significant experiences and reflecting on experience in the light of the Gospel.

The *GDC* advocates, in the first evangelization of the pre-catechumenate or pre-catechesis, proclaiming the Gospel in close connection with the ways in which the good news of Jesus satisfies the desires of the human heart. Biblical catechesis draws connections between present-day life and biblical characters, such as the people of Israel, Jesus, and his disciples. The Creed is explained in ways that show how great faith themes are "sources of life and light for the human being." Moral catechesis promotes "the Beatitudes as the spirit that must permeate the Decalogue," rooting human experiences "in the human virtues present in the heart of man." Liturgical catechesis makes "constant reference to the great human experiences represented by the signs and symbols of liturgical actions originating in Jewish and Christian culture" (117).

Adaptation to Culture and Situation

The implications for methodology in Catholic parishes and schools are many, for culture, broadly defined, can include not only racial and ethnic identity, but also age, gender, location, and a host of other characteristics. If we fail to communicate the Christian message in a way that it can be properly heard and understood, we have compromised not only the methodology but also the message, because the end result is that the learner understands something other than the authentic Word of God. If our message is unclear or misunderstood due to cultural differences, we have not communicated the truth. According to the *GDC*, God's revelation of his truths in human language "implies for catechesis the never-ending task of finding a language capable of communicating the word of God and the creed of the Church, which is its development, in the various circumstances of those who hear it" (146).

Accommodation for Special Needs

Out of the realization of God's willingness to accommodate for our needs, and recognition of the gifts that persons with disabilities offer to our Christian community, catechists must be willing to exert considerable effort to ensure that each person, regardless of disability or circumstance, has an opportunity to hear the message. Disabilities may include physical barriers to full participation in catechetical sessions, emotional or mental health issues, or cognitive problems that may present obstacles to understanding or articulating beliefs to others.

Our Christian faith calls us to see issues of disability with different eyes than those of the secular world. Our faith is one of paradox and mystery — our salvation was brought about through Christ's death. Jesus teaches that those who appear to be the least among us are the greatest in the kingdom of heaven. As Catholics, we cannot see persons with disabilities as less valuable or less worthy of our best catechetical efforts. The *GDC* states: "Every Christian community considers those who suffer handicaps, physical or mental, as well as other forms of disability — especially children — as persons particularly beloved of the Lord. A growth in social and ecclesial consciousness, together with undeniable progress in specialized pedagogy, makes it possible for the family and other formative centers to provide adequate catechesis for these people, who, as baptized, have this right and, if non-baptized, because they are called to salvation" (189).

Lack of educational, developmental, or economic opportunities, or difficult life circumstances, may also impose barriers to understanding the message of faith. We are called by the Church to work to include individuals in these situations as well:

> The catechesis of the marginalized must be considered within the same perspective. It addresses itself to immigrants, refugees, nomads, traveling people, the chronically ill, drug addicts, prisoners. (*GDC*, 190)

Related to these needs is a need for a renewed appreciation of the basic truth that all persons have gifts, and all have areas of need. While some needs may be more visible or readily apparent, each of us has challenges that allow us to work together as the body of Christ. As members of the Christian community, none of us is fully complete without the Body of Christ. Likewise, we all bring talents and strengths that we can offer as gifts to the Church. In choosing a disciple to lead the Church when he returns to the Father, Jesus is willing to look beyond Peter's impulsivity (and indeed to see Peter's energy and emotion as a gift that will give him the stamina and boldness he needs to lead the Church under persecution). This calls us to look past the disabilities of others and see their gifts, which at times may be hidden in the same qualities we had considered limitations.

As ministers in the Church, we too should be committed to do the unexpected, the inconvenient — even the radical — to ensure that everyone has a chance to meet Jesus. Just as the friends of the man who could not walk cut a hole in the roof so that their friend could meet Jesus and be healed, we should be ready to go out of our way to ensure that physical disabilities never keep someone from hearing the Gospel. Our parishes — likewise Catholic schools — should, to the extent possible, make accommodations for special needs.

Like Phillip, those who catechize should be willing to take extra time to help persons with disabilities that cause them to have difficulty understanding or sharing the message. They should work one-on-one with them, if necessary, to ensure that they too may respond to the Gospel. But when possible, the extra assistance given to persons with learning difficulties should be offered in the context of the larger community (see below). Likewise, we should help our brothers and sisters in the parish, as a whole, grow in their understanding of persons with disabilities — their needs and their gifts.

The section on catechesis for persons with disabilities in the United States *National Directory for Catechesis* begins with the following quote from the U.S. bishops' previous statement, *Welcome and Justice for Persons with Disabilities*: "We are a single flock under the care of a single shepherd. There can be no separate Church for persons with disabilities" (1).

The bishops go on to point out the valuable contributions to Church life and leadership that have been made by persons with disabilities, and our responsibility to meet their catechetical needs. In the *National Directory for Catechesis*, strong emphasis is placed on full inclusion of persons with disabilities in every aspect of parish life, including celebration of the sacraments (see paragraph 36, sec. 3b-3) and participation in faith formation:

> Persons with disabilities should be integrated into ordinary catechetical programs as much as possible.... They should not be segregated for specialized catechesis unless their disabilities make it impossible for them to participate in the basic catechetical program. (49)

Meeting the specialized needs of persons with disabilities can sometimes pose a challenge to catechists and catechetical leaders. Here are some initial steps for catechists, catechetical leaders, and other teachers of the faith:

- **Begin by listening.** The *NDC* recommends a personalized approach that involves listening to persons with disabilities and their families. This is the best way to find out about both the strengths and the needs present.

- In keeping with Catholic teaching on the dignity of all human persons, **realize that persons with disabilities have an identity that extends beyond their disability.** Care must be taken to avoid both the language and the thinking that identifies individuals solely based on their disability — for example, "a quadriplegic" or "a schizo-phrenic." Instead, we should use language that reflects our recognition that a person is more than his or her disability, that the disability is one characteristic among many — for example, "a person with quadriplegia" or "a person with schizophrenia." This is called *"person-first language,"* because it names the person first, and then the disability.

- **Recognize that each person has strengths and areas of need.** Some strengths and needs are more visible to us than others, but reflecting on the ways in which we sometimes need help can assist catechists in experiencing solidarity with their sisters and brothers with disabilities and appreciating the gifts they can bring to our communities.

- **Basic education about disabilities and appropriate learning modifications can help the catechist feel more confident and comfortable in his or her interactions with individuals with disabilities.** For example, a catechist working with a child who has been diagnosed with a reading disability may wish to do some research on learning modifications that are commonly effective for children with reading difficulties. Again, however, it is important to remember that each individual is unique, and one must never assume that one knows the needs of a person with disabilities without first listening to that individual and his or her family.

Questions for Reflection

- How does the catechetical methodology used in your parish or school assist learners in seeing their personal experiences in the light of faith?

- In what ways does your parish or school make adaptations for the diversity of cultures and situational contexts that your learners bring?

- What accommodations are made for persons with special needs? In what ways do persons with special needs also contribute their own gifts to the community?

Chapter 4

God's Pedagogy Is Incarnational

Unity of Words and Deeds

As the old cliché goes, "Actions speak louder than words." Certainly, in our contemporary culture, we want to see words backed up by action if we are to believe what the words say. If the words and actions don't go together, we call it hypocritical.

The Vatican II *Dogmatic Constitution on Divine Revelation*, known by its Latin name *Dei Verbum,* points out the "inner unity" of deeds and words in God's plan of revelation: "The deeds wrought by God in the history of salvation manifest and confirm the teaching and realities signified by the words, while the words proclaim the deeds and clarify the mystery contained in them" (2). From speaking the universe into existence, to his promise to Noah and his covenants with Abraham and Moses, to the Word made flesh in Jesus Christ, it is evident that God's word becomes action.

God wants that same unity of words and deeds to be expressed in the lives of each Christian. Through our baptism, we have put on Christ. We have been baptized into his death and raised with him to new life. Yet, as Saint Paul says, this new life is Christ living in us. Therefore, although the Law of Moses, which was fulfilled in Christ, no longer binds us, we still have responsibility as disciples of Christ — the responsibility to put our faith into action. It is God's grace, received through faith, that saves us. Yet, this is not "cheap grace," as the German theologian Dietrich Bonhoeffer called it in *The Cost of Discipleship* (first published in 1937), in which we understand God's grace to mean his unconditional mercy and forgiveness, and then assume that we have no responsibility whatsoever. Rather, Scripture tells us, "faith of itself, if it does not have works, is dead" (Jas 2:17).

The Christian community is called to continue Christ's unity of words and deeds by providing a "living catechesis"(*GDC*, 141). We have especially recognized the great example that is given to us in the saints, who allowed God's word to take root in their lives and produce heroic Christian virtue. We are called to cooperate with the grace God gives us, a grace that enables us to follow Christ and live as the people God made us to be. This *spirituality of discipleship* is especially important in the lives of catechists, who are called not only to be disciples, but also to "make disciples" (Mt 28:19).

Speaking about the Eucharist, Saint Augustine taught his followers: "Receive what you are. Become what you receive." As Christians, we are all parts of the Body of Christ, and as we receive the Body of Christ in the Eucharist, we are called to form ourselves more and more to the image of Christ in our everyday actions. God forms us by allowing us to grow in holy action through his gift of sanctifying grace, "a stable and supernatural disposition that perfects the soul itself to enable it to live with

God, to act by his love" (*Catechism*, 2000). If we have authentic faith and are responding to God's grace, good works will grow in our lives. In the previously quoted passed from James, he goes on to say the following:

> Indeed someone might say, "You have faith and I have works." Demonstrate your faith to me without works, and I will demonstrate my faith to you from my works. (2:17-18)

God's Holy Spirit, dwelling within the hearts of the faithful, serves as pedagogue, instructing the Christian in the ways of God, and the gifts of the Spirit bear visible fruits: charity, joy, peace, patience, kindness, goodness, generosity, gentleness, faithfulness, modesty, self-control, and chastity (see *Catechism*, 1832; Gal 5:22-23).

A Pedagogy of the Senses

God desires to enter into relationship with humanity. From the very beginning of time, he has revealed himself to men and women in a variety of ways. *Dei Verbum* states that God "gives men an enduring witness to Himself in created realities" (3). Saint Paul points out that God reveals himself in creation itself: "Ever since the creation of the world, his invisible attributes of eternal power and divinity have been able to be understood and perceived in what he has made" (Rom 1:20). Jesus himself taught not only through words, but also through his healings and other miracles, and his compassionate example as he cared for the poor and marginalized.

As he taught about God's kingdom, Jesus frequently cited visible illustrations of what he was teaching. For example, on an occasion when he was teaching his disciples about humility, he brought a small child for them to see as an example of what God wants us, spiritually, to be (see Mt 18:1-6). Jesus was a keen observer of his environment, and he watched for concrete examples of the principles he wanted his disciples to live.

> Jesus perfected revelation by fulfilling it through his whole work of making Himself present and manifesting Himself: through His words and deeds, His signs and wonders, but especially through His death and glorious resurrection from the dead and final sending of the Spirit of truth. (*Dei Verbum*, 4)

Early Christian teachers followed Christ's example of multi-sensory methodology. Saint Paul, for example, taught both by preaching and the written word. He also used visual aids at times to engage his listeners — for example, the previously mentioned altar to an "Unknown God" (Acts 17:23). The Church continued a tradition of multi-sensory methodology, developing the signs of sacramental rites as well as using music and the visual arts to tell the Gospel story. The Church has enjoyed a rich history of painting, sculpture, music, and dramatic arts. Masterpieces like the works of Michelangelo testify to the importance that has been placed on this multi-sensory tradition. In recent decades, Catholic films and television programs have been produced to teach others about the faith. In Mass today (particularly on feast days), we might have the opportunity to smell incense, hear music, view beautiful icons and stained-glass windows, move into various prayer postures — for example, kneeling and standing — and even taste Jesus as we receive the Host and chalice.

Christocentric

The unity of God's words and deeds, the Incarnation of his revelation, is seen most fully in the person of Jesus Christ. "In these last days, he spoke to us through a son, whom he made heir of all things and through whom he created the universe, who is the refulgence of his glory, the very imprint of his being, and who sustains all things by his mighty word" (Heb 1:2-3). As Willey (2009) points out, Christ himself, on the road to Emmaus, explains "how all of the Scriptures have reference to Christ and find their fulfillment in him."

Everything God had to teach us, everything he wanted to say, was fully revealed in the person of Jesus Christ. This is why Jesus says, "Whoever has seen me has seen the Father" (Jn 14:9).

Questions for Reflection

- How has God revealed himself to you through your senses? What have you seen and experienced through Creation that speaks of the mystery and power of God?

- How does the Church today continue to use multi-sensory methodology to teach the truth of God and make us aware of his presence?

- In what way is Jesus Christ the "fullness of God's revelation" to humankind?

Chapter 5

An Incarnational Catechesis

Unity of Words and Deeds

As followers of Jesus Christ, all catechists are called to enflesh the Gospel message in their own lives. The *General Directory for Catechesis* says it this way:

> The pedagogy of God can be said to be completed when the disciple shall "become the perfect Man, fully mature with the fullness of Christ himself" (Eph 4:13). For this reason there cannot be teachers of the faith other than those who are convinced and faithful disciples of Christ and his Church. (142)

In a similar way, catechesis should also assist others in putting the faith into action. Catechetical sessions should include opportunities to reflect on the application of faith to particular situations and actions through which the learner may be salt and light in today's world. In this way, the catechist inspires a

unity of words and deeds in those being catechized, inspiring a
Church of believers who put their faith, the faith of the apostles,
into action in the world today:

> The words of the holy fathers witness to the presence
> of this living tradition, whose wealth is poured into the
> practice and life of the believing and praying Church.
> Through the same tradition the Church's full canon
> of the sacred books is known, and the sacred writings
> themselves are more profoundly understood and un-
> ceasingly made active in her. (*Dei Verbum*, 8)

Pedagogy of the Senses

Following the multi-sensory pedagogy of God, as catechists we
should employ a variety of methods according to the needs and
the interests of those we catechize. The *General Directory for
Catechesis* states, "Perfect fidelity to Catholic doctrine is compatible with a rich diversity of presentation" (122). The *GDC*
goes on to say, "The 'variety of methods is a sign of life and richness' as well as a demonstration of respect for those to whom
catechesis is addressed" (148). This speaks to the importance of
developmentally appropriate catechesis, teaching the faith with
an awareness of what people need and enjoy at various ages and
stages of development, and using methods that fit the developmental level one is catechizing. Another way in which our
variety of methods can show respect for those being catechized
is the way in which the activities we use reflect an understanding of the various abilities and learning styles that exist within a
group — even a group of same-age peers.

Three decades ago, an idea emerged that shed new insight on how individuals learn. In his 1993 book, *Frames of Mind*, Harvard University psychologist Dr. Howard Gardner proposed a new theory of intelligence, called the "Theory of Multiple Intelligences." Gardner asserted that there was not just one type of intelligence, but many.

The *Theory of Multiple Intelligences* eventually made its way into educational methodology in general, and more recently has found its place in discussions about catechesis. This theory provides us with an excellent framework for thinking about meeting the multiple learning needs present among those we catechize. Refusing to adapt our methodologies in ways that are multi-sensory is like saying that only persons with particular types of abilities and interests should have access to the Christian faith. Using only the typical methods of reading and writing implies that only those high in linguistic intelligence can understand the Gospel. This is, of course, untrue. The Gospel is for everyone, and it needs to be communicated in ways that result in real understanding, reflection, and application. There are important reasons, therefore, to *use multi-sensory methodology* — activities that use various senses and abilities.

Here is a list of Gardner's eight multiple intelligences, and some suggestions for their application to catechesis:

- **Linguistic Intelligence:** the ability to read, write, or speak well. Dr. Martin Luther King Jr., who gave energetic and inspirational speeches, was high in linguistic intelligence. Those who are high in linguistic intelligence will learn best from reading, writing, speaking, storytelling, poetry, and creative writing.

- **Spatial Intelligence:** the ability to read charts, graphs, and diagrams, or to excel in the visual arts, such as painting, drawing, or photography. Great artists such as Leonardo da Vinci are high in spatial intelligence. In catechetical sessions, those who are high in spatial intelligence may benefit from visuals such as a Bible timeline, visual media such as movie clips, or other visual aids such as pictures, icons, and statues.

- **Logical-Mathematical Intelligence:** the ability to use numbers and logic, to solve puzzles, or to use the scientific method. Albert Einstein is one individual we would recognize as being high in logical-mathematical intelligence. Those high in logical-mathematical intelligence will benefit from puzzles, riddles, or brainteasers to introduce a lesson's theme. They may also enjoy logical arguments for the faith, such as those laid out by Saint Thomas Aquinas in the *Summa Theologica*. These individuals will likely be fascinated by typology in Scripture, for example, exploring the relationship between the Ark of the Covenant and the Virgin Mary, whom the Church Fathers called the "Ark of the New Covenant," or seeing the connection between the good king and priest Melchizedek in the Old Testament and Jesus Christ, who was king and high priest.

- **Musical/Rhythmic Intelligence:** skill at singing, playing an instrument, and appreciating or composing music. Great composers such as Bach and Beethoven were high in musical intelligence. Individuals who are high in musical intelligence will be drawn to opportunities to sing, play instruments, or engage in prayerful meditation set to music.

- **Bodily-kinesthetic Intelligence:** skill at using the whole body in physical movement or hands-on learning activities. Great athletes, such as major-league sports stars and Olympic medalists are high in bodily-kinesthetic intelligence. Acting could also be considered an activity that draws on bodily-kinesthetic intelligence, since body language and facial expressions are so central to dramatic presentations. Individuals who are high in bodily-kinesthetic intelligence will likely benefit from methods that employ movement, participation in dramatization of Scripture stories or scenes from the life of a saint, and other hands-on activities.

- **Naturalist Intelligence:** sensitivity to the features of the natural world; the ability to discriminate between various types of living things. The late Steve Irwin (the "Crocodile Hunter") and Jane Goodall, who worked with primates, were both high in naturalist intelligence. Persons with naturalist intelligence will enjoy opportunities to explore God's creation, to have catechetical sessions or activities outside, to go on walks for prayerful meditation, or to participate in outdoor Stations of the Cross. They may also benefit from object lessons and examples related to the natural world.

- **Interpersonal Intelligence:** the ability to relate to various types of people, to work in groups, and get along with others. Pope John Paul II, who appealed to so many different types of people, and was known for being both personable and sensitive to others, was high in interpersonal intelligence. These individuals will thrive in a catechetical setting when they have opportunities to participate in cooperative group activities and service projects and to be a part of group discussions.

- **Intrapersonal Intelligence:** skill at introspection and contemplation. Great Catholic mystics such as Saint Teresa of Avila are high in intrapersonal intelligence. These individuals benefit from independent work, introspection and reflection, contemplative prayer, and journaling.

Christocentric

All of the different methodologies we use have a common purpose — fostering a relationship with Jesus. "The definitive aim of catechesis is to put people not only in touch but in communion, in intimacy, with Jesus Christ" (*Catechesi Tradendae*, 5). The message of Christ is at the center of the ministry of catechesis, because in him, God has fully revealed himself:

The fact that Jesus Christ is the fullness of Revelation is the foundation for the "Christocentricity" of catechesis: the mystery of Christ, in the revealed message, is not another element alongside others, it is rather the center from which all other elements are structured and illuminated. (*General Directory for Catechesis*, 41).

The person of Jesus Christ is the central content of catechesis. Scripture, Sacred Tradition, and the teaching of the Magisterium all serve to illuminate the person of Christ and foster relationship with him.

Questions for Reflection

- How are you an example to others, especially those you catechize?

- In what ways is your current catechesis multi-sensory?

- How might you incorporate more multi-sensory elements for visual, auditory, and kinesthetic learners?

- In what ways does your process of catechizing emphasize the centrality of Christ's incarnation?

Chapter 6

God's Pedagogy Is Relational

"GOD IS LOVE" (1 Jn 4:8), and he has created us to love and serve him and one another. God teaches us these truths through relationship with himself and with others. God initiates this relationship with us through the desire for God that is written into the human heart (*Catechism of the Catholic Church*, 27). God seeks and welcomes us as friends, desiring to enter into intimate relationship with each of us:

> Through this revelation, therefore, the invisible God (see Col 1:15; 1 Tm 1:17) out of the abundance of His love speaks to men as friends (see Ex 33:11; Jn 15:14-15) and lives among them (see Bar 3:38), so that He may invite and take them into fellowship with Himself. (*Dei Verbum*, 2)

A Communion of Persons

God's nature is one of love and communion, for the Holy Trinity is a communion of persons, three, yet mysteriously one. It is God's plan to teach us about his communal nature from the very beginning of our lives, for he has designed the family as a communion of persons as well (*Catechism*, 2205). God the Father and God the Son give themselves fully and completely to one another, and the spirit of love between them becomes another person — the Holy Spirit. In God's plan for marriage, the fruit of the love between husband and wife is potentially another person — a child.

Christ and the Church

God also chose the family, and marriage in particular, to reveal to us the mystery of his relationship with humankind, specifically the relationship between Christ and his Church (see Eph 5:21-33). Husband and wife are called to offer themselves to one another in self-giving love, and in doing so they both model and experience the relationship between God and his people.

It is because of the family's role as sources of ecclesial communion and divine revelation that we refer to the family as a "domestic church" (*Lumen Gentium*, 11). Parents are the first and most important teachers of their children in the ways of the Lord (*General Directory for Catechesis*, 226).

The Ecclesial Community as Family

The larger Church is also designed by God as a family, with God as Father (see Eph 4:6). By virtue of our baptism, we are adopted as sons and daughters of God (Rom 8:14-17) and live as brothers and sisters in Christ. This familial character of the people of God is important in two ways. First, God chooses to reveal himself to us as Father, using the human experiences of parenthood and childhood to help us understand God and our relationship with him. (One may even go so far as to assume that God created marriage and parenthood to reveal these truths.) Second, God establishes the community of faith as a family, a communion of persons, showing us that we need one another to make this journey. Consistent with this, Jesus sends his disciples to teach in groups of two (Mk 6:7).

At the Last Supper, he clearly expresses his will that his followers continue to grow in communion with one another, stating: "I give you a new commandment: love one another. As I have loved you, so you also should love one another" (Jn 13:34). The command to love one's neighbor was not a new commandment, as Jesus had previously spoken at length on this (see Lk 10:25-37). Therefore, this "new commandment" to love one another implies something more than merely showing love or mercy to another. Rather, one may argue that Jesus intended to call his disciples to a *relationship* of mutual self-gift.

In his apostolic letter *Novo Millenio Inuente*, subtitled *At the Close of the Great Jubilee of the Year 2000*, Pope John Paul II discussed the spirituality of communion that he believed was the great task awaiting the Church in the new millennium. He said the following:

> To make the Church *the home and the school of communion*: that is the great challenge facing us in the millennium which is now beginning, if we wish to be faithful to God's plan and respond to the world's deepest yearnings. (43, emphasis in original)

Pope John Paul II considered further the following to be key aspects of this *spirituality of communion*:

- "The heart's contemplation of the mystery of the Trinity dwelling in us, and whose light we must also be able to see shining on the face of the brothers and sisters around us."

- The "ability to think of our brothers and sisters in faith within the profound unity of the Mystical Body, and therefore as 'those who are a part of me.' This makes us able to share their joys and sufferings, to sense their desires and attend to their needs, to offer them deep and genuine friendship."

- "The ability to see what is positive in others, to welcome it and prize it as a gift from God."

- "To know how to 'make room' for our brothers and sisters, bearing 'each other's burdens' (Gal 6:2)."

Pope John Paul was so certain that this path was vital to the future of the Church that he further stated: "Let us have no illusions: unless we follow this spiritual path, external structures of communion will serve very little purpose. They would become mechanisms without a soul, 'masks' of communion rather than its means of expression and growth" (43).

Aspects of Community Life

The early Church placed a high priority on functioning as a community, and Scripture describes early Christians as being "together" and having "all things in common" (Acts 2:44). The cohesiveness of their community helped them to face extreme persecution and fulfill Christ's mandate: "Go into the whole world and proclaim the gospel to the every creature" (Mk 16:15).

Because humans are social by nature, the good of each individual, according to the *Catechism*, is related to the common good (1905). The Second Vatican Council defined "common good" as "the sum of those conditions of social life which allow social groups and their individual members relatively thorough and ready access to their own fulfillment" (*Gaudium et Spes*, 26).

The common good presupposes "respect for the person" (*Catechism*, 1907), "requires the social well-being and development of the group itself" (1908), and requires peace, or "the stability and security of a just order" (1909).

The *General Directory of Catechesis* draws on the teachings of Christ to list several attitudes that are necessary for living in community. The first is "the spirit of simplicity and humility" (86). To form a close community, we must approach others without conceit or arrogance. We must recognize that God gives everyone special gifts, and not consider ourselves as better than anyone else. We must become willing to serve one another in love.

A second essential in community life is special concern for the least among us. Lewis Thomas, a researcher at Tulane Univeristy, said, "A society can be judged by the way it treats its most disadvantaged, its least beloved." Jesus said, "Whatever you did for one of these least brothers of mine, you did for me" (Mt 25:40). We must recognize and appreciate the dignity present in each member of society and see each person as a unique being, created in God's image. We must work to meet the needs of all, especially basic needs such as food, shelter, safety, education, and health care. A similar requirement of community life

is a concern for the marginalized, those who have been alien-
ated or who have gone astray. When we see ourselves as the one
body described in Scripture (see 1 Cor 12:12-27), we will not
feel whole when one of our members is separated from us.

When we truly care for one another, we do not cover up
wounds that need to be healed, or turn our backs when someone is engaging in destructive behavior. Being loving sometimes requires us to be painfully honest, to warn others of the
harm they are doing to themselves or others, and to help them
do better.

Common prayer is another quality of Christian community life. In communal prayer, we approach God with one voice,
making our needs known to one another and to the Creator
who gives us every good thing. Praying together helps us to better discern God's will for our lives and opens the community to
the work of the Holy Spirit.

In any group of human beings, people are bound to have
hurt feelings or misunderstandings. An attitude of mutual forgiveness and reconciliation is essential for living in communion
with one another, so essential, in fact, that Jesus stated, "If you
bring you gift to the altar, and there recall that your brother has
anything against you, leave your gift there at the altar, go first
and be reconciled with your brother, and then come and offer
your gift" (Mt 5:23-24). We should approach God after we have
made efforts to be reconciled with one another, for God for-
gives us as we forgive others (see Mt 6:14).

All of these important features of community life can be
summarized, according to the *General Directory for Catechesis*,
in an attitude of love for one another. When we love one another as God has loved us, we can withstand almost any obstacles,
"because love covers a multitude of sins" (1 Pt 4:8).

Community and Ecumenism

Our awareness of the qualities of Christian community should lead us to pursue unity with those in other Christian traditions. This pursuit of unity begins with a clear knowledge of the faith we profess, but also an understanding for the beliefs of others. In our pursuit of unity, we must not compromise what we believe to be essential truth in an effort to get along with one another, for such compromise is not true unity of faith. However, we should work to discover and celebrate the beliefs we share in common, praying for the day that God will lead us to an even deeper communion with himself and one another.

The next chapter will explore how we might begin to foster a spirituality of communion, particularly in our catechesis, beginning in the domestic church — the individual families of our parishes — and extending beyond that to the larger Christian community.

Questions for Reflection

- What are the characteristics of a community?

- When have you experienced a true sense of communion in your family? In the Church?

Chapter 7

A RELATIONAL CATECHESIS

THE IMPLICATIONS OF GOD'S RELATIONAL PEDAGOGY are numerous. First, we are called to consider the importance of relationship with those we catechize, beginning with the way in which we engage them. God begins by reaching out to us, not by waiting for us to come to him. This speaks to the importance of efforts to evangelize not only our families and parishes, but also the whole world in which we live. Second, as God enters into dialogue with us, we are called to follow this example by providing catechesis that "is rooted in interpersonal relations and makes its own the process of dialogue" (*GDC*, 143).

Catechesis is an apprenticeship in the Christian life (*GDC*, 30,56). Learning, an apprenticeship, takes place primarily in the context of the relationship between the mentor and the apprentice. The catechist has a responsibility to know the person being catechized — the context of their lives, their interests, gifts, and challenges. Every person is unique and unrepeatable, and God calls each of us by name. Therefore, there is no one-size-fits-all approach to catechesis. Entering into relationship with those we catechize, and fostering relationships within the Christian community, help us to communicate God's love for each person and our love for one another. It is this call to love that is the central message of Jesus Christ.

The primacy of the family in God's pedagogy calls us to a catechesis that both supports and involves the family to the greatest extent possible. The family has a privileged place in catechesis. The *Catechism* states that "parents receive the responsibility of evangelizing their children" and calls them the "first heralds" of the faith (2225).

Today, catechetical leaders face several challenges with regard to engaging the family. These challenges include hectic schedules and divided attention, which have become more problematic over the last few decades. One study from the University of Michigan showed that in the years between 1981 and 1997, there was a shocking decrease in the amount of time devoted solely to family conversation, a 33 percent decrease in families eating dinner together, and a 28 percent drop in family vacations. In the same period, the time children spent in structured sports doubled, and passive spectator leisure time increased fivefold. More recently, a study by the Annenberg Center for the Digital Future at the University of Southern California showed that 28 percent of Americans say they are spending less time with their families than in the previous year, and this rise appears to be related to more time on digital media, such as Facebook, Twitter, and the Internet in general.

Another challenge to engaging the family is the increasing secularization of modern society, which can lead to a compartmentalization of faith so that it is seen as an extracurricular activity rather than a central aspect of one's life that impacts all others. A third challenge is the fact that many adults are poorly formed in their faith due to incomplete or inadequate catechesis, or a "confirmation as graduation" mentality that precluded continuing faith formation as an adult. Consequently, these adults may lack the confidence and/or knowledge to guide their families in the faith. Finally, there exists a cultural fear of commitment, likely due to the busyness of modern life — a struggle with taking on additional responsibilities.

Family-Friendly Grade-Level Catechetical Programs

Parish-based grade-level catechesis can be made more family friendly by choosing texts that provide practical and creative ways to involve families and using the programs in a manner that is responsive to the needs of today's families.

- Choose a grade-level textbook series with a strong family component — for example, one that includes a section written specifically for families as part of each lesson. At minimum, this should include information about the doctrinal material the child has learned, developmental information about how children this age understand the topic, adult-level catechesis for the parents, and practical ways families can share the message at home. These pages can and should be perforated, so they can be sent home each week if the textbooks stay at the parish. Other strong family components, such as online resources for families and materials to assist in family prayer, would be helpful as well.

- Involve parents as volunteers, and give them plenty of options with respect to roles. Sometimes parents may be left to feel as if they can only help with the parish catechetical program if they feel called and equipped to be catechists, but parents could also volunteer as classroom assistants, helpers with special events, or "guest speakers" to discuss other areas of ministry in which they are involved. For example, parents who serve as extraordinary ministers of holy Communion could help instruct the children preparing for first Communion on the proper way to receive. In this type of model, the director or coordinator of religious education becomes more of a coordinator and facilitator of adult volunteers, so it's essential to have someone in this role that can work effectively with adults and offer them appropriate formation.

- Where possible, order lessons so that multiple children from the same family are working on the same themes at the same times of the year. This makes it easier for families to learn together.

- Provide intergenerational experiences. Many parishes have found a transition to a program of intergenerational catechesis alone to be impractical or imprudent, but a traditional grade-level program can be greatly enhanced by adding intergenerational events and experiences. Consider adding seasonal celebrations for All Saints' Day, the feast day of your parish's patron saint, and perhaps for Advent and Lent. For children preparing for the sacraments, host daylong retreats that are designed for the whole family, with perhaps some time for parents and children separately and some opportunities for experiences together.

Family-Sensitive Adult Formation

We can increase participation in adult formation as well when we take some steps to be more family sensitive:

- Offer a variety of adult-formation classes and experiences that allow adults to choose based on their interest and phase of life. Many Protestant churches offer adult classes for various groups, such as singles, young professionals, older adults, etc.

- Make adult formation practical. Offer topics that intersect with the dally life of the adult learner, such as being a faithful Catholic in the workplace, raising Catholic kids and teens, and other real-life concerns.

- Make adult formation available and practical for families. Consider offering adult classes at the same time as children's classes, when adults are already coming to the parish. Offer child care for younger children.

Pope John Paul II famously said, "As the family goes, so goes society, and so goes the world in which we live." We could just as easily say, "As the family goes, so goes the parish, and so goes the Church in which we live" — for our parishes are made up of families, and every child with a vocation to the priesthood and religious life is born within a family. For this reason, Pope Benedict XVI said, "The family … is the 'cradle' of life and of every vocation" (Angelus, February 4, 2007). Let us renew our commitment to place families at the center of our catechetical efforts.

Formation for Family Life

In a related vein, catechetical programs in Catholic parishes and schools should help in forming the human person for relationship by offering sound teaching on communication, interpersonal problem-solving skills, human sexuality and chastity, and the Sacrament of Matrimony. Following the recommendation of Pope John Paul II, educational programs should include remote, proximate, and immediate preparation for marriage and family life (*Familiaris Consortio*, 66).

Remote preparation occurs throughout childhood and includes, first and foremost, all that a child learns through the parent-child relationship and through observation of and participation in the interactions of others in the home. Programs of catechetical formation have a role in this process insofar as they form parents to set good examples for their children and guide them appropriately. Catechetical programs will also assist in organizing and articulating what a child learns in the home about charity, relationships with others, and the Sacrament of Matrimony. Proximate preparation begins around the time of puberty and represents a more intensive effort to educate the child about relationships, chastity, and discerning a vocation to married life. This formation should necessarily occur in cooperation with parents, for, as in all catechesis of children, the parents are the primary teachers. However, in the case of matters related to human sexuality, the role of parents is even more critical, for three reasons.

First, it is the clear and definitive teaching of the Church that parents should be the primary sexuality educators of their children. The U.S. bishops, in their document *Human Sexuality: A Catholic Perspective for Education and Lifelong Learning*, state: "It is appropriate that education in human sexuality find its primary locus within the family context.... The Congregation for Catholic Education suggests that with regard to the more intimate aspects of sexuality, whether biological or affective, an individual education is desirable, preferably within the sphere of the family" (p. 71). Likewise, the Pontifical Council for the Family states, "any educative activity, related to education for love and carried out by persons outside the family, must be subject to parents' acceptance of it and must be seen not as a substitute but as a support for their work" (*Truth and Meaning of Human Sexuality*, 113).

Second, research evidence makes it clear parents need to be involved. In 2001, the National Campaign to Prevent Teen Pregnancy in Washington, D.C., conducted a national survey of adults and teens. Critical differences were noted between what teens think and what adults assume teens think. When asked about the most influential factor in teen sexual decision-making, teens reported that their parents were the single most influential factor. Adults wrongly assumed that their children's peers had the greatest influence. Other studies also support this finding (Karofsky, Zeng, Kosorok, 2000; Resnick, Bearman, Blum, et al., 1997; Dilorio, Kelley, Hockenberry-Eaton, 1999). Teens who feel close to their parents are much less likely to engage in risky behavior (Jaccard, Dittus, Gordon, 2000). Teens with parents who express disapproval of nonmarital sex and contraceptive use are less likely than their peers to have sex (Lederman, Chan, Roberts-Gray, 2004). Teens who talk to a parent about sex tend to wait to have sex, have fewer sexual partners, and are more likely to name a parent than a peer as a good source of information about sex (Whitaker, Miller, 2000).

And third, partnering with parents helps to avoid misunderstanding and/or scandal. When parents and catechists have a relationship of clear communication and collaboration, parents are well informed about the content covered in catechetical sessions and have a stronger sense of their own responsibilities in the home.

The Larger "Family" of the Parish and Worldwide Church

Catechetical programs should promote an understanding of the parish community as family, providing a catechesis that "values the community experience of faith, which is proper to the people of God, the Church" (*GDC*, 143).

Whenever possible, catechetical sessions should model this sense of interconnectedness, perhaps by being team-led and at all times presenting catechetical material in a manner that is in communion with the teaching office of the Church. We are also connected, at least in some sense, with all Christian people around the world, and with all those who profess a belief in God. It is important that our catechetical activities always convey respect for those who believe differently than we do.

Children begin learning about living in communities from the very beginning of their lives. The first community they experience is the family. Later, they experience community through their schools, neighborhoods, and parishes. Making learning about community explicit, by talking about and demonstrating how we should treat one another, and working to identify and meet each group member's needs, should be a priority for catechists working with any age level.

As children grow, their community of peers becomes more and more important in their lives. Even more emphasis should be placed on the community experience of faith from the pre-teen years on through adulthood. Here are a few suggestions for fostering a sense of community in catechetical sessions:

- Even if your sessions are only an hour long, allow a few minutes of community-oriented "gathering time" at the beginning of each group session. For children, this may include activities they can do together, such as religious-themed puzzles or games (available at many Christian bookstores). Older teens and adults are generally comfortable making conversation as they gather, especially when refreshments are provided.

- During group times, engage participants in conversation about what is happening in their lives. Ask if they (or someone in their family) needs prayers, and include these intentions during group prayer times.

- Invite ministry leaders in your parish to come to the catechetical session and talk with the participants about how the work they do contributes to the parish community.

Questions for Reflection

- What am I doing right now to honor the "privileged place" of family in catechesis? How can I involve families more in the work I do?

- How is our catechetical program promoting a sense of the larger community of faith, both in our parish and around the world?

Chapter 8

God's Pedagogy Is Structured, Systematic, Comprehensive

"God, in his greatness, uses a pedagogy to reveal himself to the human person: he uses human events and words to communicate his plan; he does so progressively and in stages, so as to draw even closer to man. God, in fact, operates in such a manner that man comes to knowledge of his salvific plan by means of the events of salvation history and the inspired words which accompany and explain them" (*GDC*, 38).

The *Catechism of the Catholic Church* discusses several "stages of revelation" in which God made himself gradually known to his people (54-65). God revealed himself to Adam and Eve, our first parents. He made a covenant with Noah expressing the "principle of the divine economy towards the 'nations'" (56). God later made a covenant with Abraham, whose descendants became God's chosen people. God freed his people from slavery in Egypt and established a covenant with them, giving them his law (62; see also Ex 19:1—20:17).

God continued to form his people Israel, and through the prophets prepared them for the coming of his Son. "Through the prophets, God forms his people in the hope of salvation, in the expectation of a new and everlasting Covenant intended for all, to be written on their hearts" (*Catechism*, 64; see also Is 2:2-4; Jer 31:31-34; Heb 10:16). *Dei Verbum* explains, "When God himself spoke to them through the mouths of the prophets, Israel daily gained a deeper and clearer understanding of His ways and made them more widely known among the nations" (14).

Jesus comes as the last and definitive revelation of God, for he is the incarnation of the complete Word of God and the Covenant established through him is everlasting (*Catechism*, 65-66). Therefore, it can be seen that God's pedagogy toward humanity is both systematic (God reveals himself over time in a step-by-step fashion as his people are ready and able to understand and accept) and comprehensive (through Jesus, God has made his revelation of himself complete). As the Church continues to interpret this complete revelation of God, she goes forth with Christ's promise that the Holy Spirit will guide her "to all truth" (Jn 16:13).

Human Development

What God does with all humankind, he also does with the individual person. The *General Directory for Catechesis* says that God "causes the person to grow progressively and patiently towards the maturity of a free son, faithful and obedient to his word" (139). Much of this maturity is based, at least in part, in the course of development of the human person. There are many aspects of human development, including:

- **Cognitive Development** — This includes growth and change in intellectual capacity and problem-solving skills. As the individual develops cognitively, he or she is able to understand increasingly difficult concepts and to apply this information to his or her everyday life.

- **Communication** — This refers to growth in the ability to process information that is taken in, as well as to express one's self. Growth in communication assists us in developing the vocabulary of faith and in expressing our faith in words, symbols, and gestures.

- **Socialization** — As we grow in empathy and knowledge of social cues and rules, we learn to form relationships and live in community. The first relationships an individual forms are usually with his or her family, and then his or her social world broadens with exposure to various social settings, including school and parish. Development in this area is important in the experience of the communal aspects of our faith, previously discussed in more detail in Chapters 6 and 7.

- **Identity** — Among the most basic questions of human existence are "Who am I?" and "Why am I here?" Identity continues to develop and change across an individual's lifespan as he or she experiences different roles. Identity development is closely connected to discerning God's plan for one's life.

- **Daily Living Skills** — Daily living skills include adaptation to various situations and the ability to have some autonomy in managing one's own affairs. A sense of autonomy is critical in an understanding of free will and our personal responsibility as human beings created in the image of God.

- **Motor Skills** — Motor skills include both the early growth of large muscles that leads to the ability to walk, run, and play, and fine motor development that brings the ability to write. The latter is an important form of expression for many individuals, including the many introspective saints that have left us profound writings on the faith.

- **Moral Development** — Growth naturally occurs in how choices are made, and how right and wrong is determined. Very young children tend to base many of their choices on whether or not the action is punished or rewarded, while as people grow they begin to have a more social sense of morality — for example, a set of guidelines agreed upon by a group — and a more internal sense of universal moral principles (those values they hold and would act upon even if those around them were doing something different). Because there is an essential moral aspect to the Christian life, moral development necessarily intersects with maturity in the faith.

- **Spiritual Development** — Individuals grow and change with respect to their sense of the spiritual and the way in which they cultivate spirituality in their lives. Saint John of the Cross discusses spiritual development in his writings, saying that it is the "beginner" who most needs external phenomena to have a spiritual experience.

- **Emotional Development** — Individuals grow in their ability to understand and regulate their emotions, as well as the ability to empathize with others, which is at the heart of feeling compassion and living as a responsible member of a community.

Structured and Disciplined

In addition, God's message is at once structured and imposes structure. It calls us to grow in self-discipline, and imposes limits and consequences, both positive and negative. God disciplines those he loves (see Heb 12:6). We sometimes associate rules and guidelines with restrictions on freedom, but God's commandments are designed to give us the freedom to be the people he made us to be. "Called to beatitude but wounded by sin, man stands in need of salvation from God. Divine help comes to him in Christ through the law that guides him and the grace that sustains him" (*Catechism*, 1949).

Gradual and Adaptive, but Not Relative

It is useful to make one additional point here regarding the truths taught by God to humankind. While God reveals himself gradually and adapts his message to various times, cultures, and situations, God does not contradict himself. Contemporary thinkers often echo the words of Pontius Pilate, who did not say, "What is *the* truth?" but said, "What *is* truth?"(Jn 18:38, emphasis added), implying that there may be no absolute truth at all.

In an era in which relativism, or even nihilism, is seen as the ultimate "truth," the Christian message is distinct: there is an ultimate truth, and it can be found.

Questions for Reflection

- What was my earliest experience of God or the Church?

- How has my understanding of faith changed over time?

Chapter 9

A STRUCTURED, SYSTEMATIC, AND COMPREHENSIVE CATECHESIS

IN ITS DISCUSSION OF THE CATECHETICAL TRADITION of the Church Fathers, the *General Directory for Catechesis* points to what it refers to as "the gradual and progressive conception of Christian formation, arranged in stages: The fathers model the catechumenate on the divine pedagogy; in the catechumenal process the catechumen, like the people of Israel, goes through a journey to arrive at the promised land: Baptismal identification with Christ" (129).

For individuals exposed to the faith in childhood, this journey necessarily has a developmental component. What is important as children learn about their faith? Not only *what* we teach, but also *how the learner receives it*. We can teach things in a theologically accurate way, but if it's not delivered in a developmentally appropriate manner, the material may be misunderstood. We can misrepresent Catholic teaching by getting the facts wrong, but we could also misrepresent Catholic teaching by delivering the facts in a way that they are not well understood. While each individual is unique, there are some general trends in development that can guide age-specific catechesis.

Catechesis in the Early Years — Preschool and Kindergarten

There are several reasons for parishes to have an early childhood religion program. First, Jesus said, "Let the children come to me, and do not prevent them; for the kingdom of heaven belongs to such as these" (Mt 19:14). Our parishes should be places of welcome for children of all ages. They need to see that there is a special place for them in their parish community.

Additionally, early childhood religion programs help to keep families engaged in the parish between the baptismal and sacramental years — a time when young families especially need the support of their parish community. Providing ongoing catechesis between baptism and first penance is one way of modeling how faith formation is to be part of one's whole life, not just during years of schooling.

Finally, and perhaps most importantly, new research is indicating that an adult's capacity for relationship with God is based in part on early childhood experiences with God and spirituality. A few years ago, there was speculation that there may be a "God gene" — a genetic predisposition for religion and spirituality. Not only are there some individuals who are drawn to this and some who aren't, but their brains even show distinct differences. Now we are learning that these differences in behaviors and even brain structures are not so much dependent on genetics as they are on early experiences. Just as the capacity for relationships with people is developed in these early years, the capacity for relationship with God needs to be nurtured in these years in order for it to reach its true potential.

Preschool and kindergarten-age children have hopefully learned from watching their parents that there is a God who made them and who made the world, but their very concrete style of thinking makes an abstract concept such as an invisible God very difficult for them. Their primary understanding of God comes from the way in which they see their parents and others praying and acknowledging God in their lives. They also discover Jesus and the saints through objects, such as icons, statues, and other concrete symbols of our faith. Stories, which are at the heart of our Judeo-Christian tradition, are another excellent tool for promoting knowledge of the faith in preschool-age children.

Catechesis in the Elementary Years

First Grade. Because this is the beginning of formal religious education for many children, and because the aim of catechesis is "communion and intimacy, with Jesus Christ" (*GDC*, 80, quoting *Catechesi Tradendae*, 5), it is logical to focus first-grade catechesis around the person of Jesus. First graders are just beginning to move beyond the developmental self-focus of the preschool years, so an introduction to relationship with Jesus and the Church community is appropriate. Children this age are beginning to move into a cognitive stage of rule-based thinking, so this is a great opportunity to provide them with the basic teachings of the faith. In the Judeo-Christian tradition, these basic teachings are often communicated in the form of stories. Interactive storytelling techniques involving visuals, three-dimensional props, and acting out the story can be especially engaging activities for children this age.

Second Grade. Children this age are in the Piagetian cognitive stage of "concrete operations." They understand cause and effect and know the world works according to rules. Therefore, this is a great time to introduce God's rules and guidelines for living. Because they have reached the age of reason, second graders are better able to understand that the Eucharist is not ordinary bread and wine, because Jesus said it was His Body and Blood. Second graders are concrete thinkers and need many hands-on activities and practical explanations. Our approach to teaching the sacraments should be step by step and very concrete. This is a good time to learn the steps of the rites, parts of the Mass, and basics of what the Church teaches about the sacraments.

Third Grade. Children this age have entered what social/developmental theorist Harry Stack Sullivan called the "chumship stage," when same-age peers become very important and children often have "best friends." For this reason, it is an ideal time to focus on the parish community. Third graders are more aware of the larger world, so this is a good time to talk about the larger worldwide Church and how it is organized. Their sense of the larger community makes this an ideal time to do some learning in pairs or cooperative groups. To do this effectively, catechists should make sure the tasks are well defined, that each participant has a unique role, and that time limits and transition times are given.

Fourth Grade. Fourth graders are beginning to internalize standards of behavior. Their consciences are growing quickly, and they are gaining a sense of "right" and "wrong" that goes beyond just what might bring them punishments or rewards. This is a great time to work with them on what it means to be disciples of Jesus. Fourth graders are good at using reasoning skills, but they still don't have a firm grasp on hypothetical reasoning. This means they have difficulty imagining things or situations they haven't experienced. Role playing or acting out making good choices in a moral dilemma will be especially effective, since all of us are more likely to do the things we practice.

Fifth Grade. Fifth graders are growing in their ability to understand symbols and signs. This makes fifth grade an ideal time to take an in-depth look at the sacraments and rites of the Church. Fifth graders are also in a stage of identity development in which they begin to seriously consider who they will be when they are older. This makes this age an important time for learning about vocation and the sacraments at the service of holy Communion. It is helpful to ask children this age to consider what God's plan for their life might be, and encourage them to seek that plan in the talents and opportunities God has given them.

Sixth Grade. Children in sixth grade are growing in their abstract-thinking ability and have made great strides in reading and writing ability. This makes sixth grade an ideal time to study sacred Scripture and begin to connect the events of salvation history. The use of Bible timelines can assist children with this. Children in sixth grade are also becoming young adolescents, so this is an important time to strengthen Catholic identity through study of our faith ancestors and basic doctrines. Studying the saints and how they articulated and defended the Catholic faith can be helpful.

Middle School. The continued physical growth during the middle-school years brings identity issues and questions. Middle-school students are often highly insecure and self-conscious. They are looking for reassurance that they are "normal" and seek a sense of belonging with others. They also want to see that the faith is relevant to them. If they cannot make connections between their faith and everyday life, they may question the importance of what they are learning in a catechetical setting. Asking about the interests of the group and being familiar with their media (music, movies, video games, etc.) can help catechists know what types of analogies and applications can best speak to the learners.

High School. High-school students are becoming more independent and autonomous, and necessarily so, since they will soon be adults who are responsible for their own lives. Many individuals this age question aspects of the faith, but appropriately handled this can be viewed as a step toward internalization of the principles with which they have been raised. Many teens need to wrestle with questions of faith in order to make the faith their own. Individuals this age are continuing to work on identity issues, and vocations can be presented in this context. Having an opportunity to meet priests, religious, and married persons, and hear about their vocational journeys, can help older teens discern where God might be calling them.

Adulthood. The Christian life is a process of continuing conversion, and, so, catechesis should continue throughout our life span. The adult years encompass many different ages and stages of life, including the young adult years, which for many individuals continue the themes of identity and vocation begun in adolescence. Depending on the path that individuals follow, they may later be in need of catechesis related to family life, mission, and/or other themes. In the later adult years, themes of legacy, looking back, and later life become prominent for many. Catechesis that is situated around these relevant life themes for adults of different stages of life may result in greater participation by a wider variety of people than more general "adult Bible studies" that are attempted in many parishes.

Structured and Comprehensive

The *General Directory for Catechesis*, quoting *Catechesi Tradendae (CT)*, states that the catechetical message has "a 'comprehensive hierarchical character' which constitutes a vital synthesis of the faith" (114; see *CT*, 31). The truths of the faith are organized in a hierarchy around the mystery of the Holy Trinity, in a Christocentric perspective. Citing the *General Catechetical Directory* (43) from the Sacred Congregation for the Clergy, the *GDC* points out that the hierarchy of truths "does not mean that some truths pertain to Faith itself less than others, but rather that some truths are based on others as of a higher priority and are illumined by them" (114).

In other words, certain truths of our faith serve as a foundation for all other teachings. These truths include the following:

1. **The Holy Trinity:** There is one God in three divine Persons — Father, Son and Holy Spirit.

2. **Jesus Christ:** The Second Person of the Holy Trinity is fully human and fully divine. He was sent by God for the salvation of humankind.

3. **The Paschal Mystery:** Jesus Christ suffered, died, was raised from the dead, and ascended to the Father.

4. **The Dignity of the Human Person:** Men and women are created in the image and likeness of God. By virtue of their creation in God's image, they have an inherent dignity.

5. **The Church:** The Church, the mystical Body of Christ, is formed, animated, and guided by the Holy Spirit. She continues Christ's ministry on earth, especially in the celebration of the seven sacraments.

Building on prior national guidelines established by the bishops, the *National Directory for Catechesis* offers several principles for the organization of catechesis in the United States, with particular applications to local churches. First, the *NDC* points out the importance of a "comprehensive pastoral plan" (58) based on the Church's mission of evangelization. This plan should help to guide catechesis at the national, diocesan, and parish level, with each level of organization respecting the competence of the other levels. For example, parishes are where most Catholics are living out their relationship with the Church, so parishes are best situated to help provide for certain aspects of the individual's everyday experience of faith, such as formation and worship.

A second principle is the "person-centered" quality of organization for catechesis. Those who are catechized and their families should be included in organizational structures.

A third principle offered by the bishops is that all Christians are responsible for catechesis. This is particularly true because of the responsibility of every Christian for evangelization and mission. This principle echoes the *General Directory for Catechesis,* which states: "In the Diocese catechesis is a unique service performed jointly by priests, deacons, religious and laity, in communion with the Bishop. The entire Christian community should feel responsible for this service" (219).

Fourth, catechetical leaders are asked to develop a statement of philosophy, goals, and basic beliefs underlying those goals. In other words, catechetical leaders should develop a mission statement for their programs so the program's guiding principles are explicit.

According to the *NDC,* when making policy decisions, organizational bodies should respect the autonomy of groups and persons most directly affected by those decisions.

The *NDC* further calls for an equitable distribution of resources for the ministry of catechesis, with more affluent parishes sharing their resources with parishes in need. Catechesis should be organized in a way that is consistent with the needs assessed and the goals stated. Assessment, planning, development, and evaluation should be continuing processes (*NDC,* 58; *GDC,* 221).

In its discussion of diocesan catechetical ministry, the *NDC* points out that collaboration is necessary not just so catechesis will be well-coordinated, but also because it "ensures a unified and coherent presentation of the faith" (59). The same could certainly be said of catechesis within the parish, because the parish is "the most important locus" of formation (*GDC,* 257). Consequently, it is vital that parish leaders collaborate with one another in catechetical activities at all levels, and collaborate with parents and families in their work with children and youth, for parents are the first educators of their children (*Catechism of the Catholic Church,* 2223).

Questions for Reflection

- How does catechesis in my community respond to the developmental needs and characteristics of persons of various ages and developmental levels?

- What is the structure of catechetical ministry in my parish, school, and/or diocese?

Chapter 10

God's Pedagogy Is Perpetual

GOD HAS ALWAYS EXISTED, and since the beginning of time has invited humanity to learn of him. God's truth, wherever it is proclaimed, perpetuates itself until it accomplishes his will. Isaiah 55:11 states, "So shall my word be that goes forth from my mouth; / It shall not return to me void, but shall do what please me, achieving the end for which I sent it."

God's truths are handed on through the generations in the forms of sacred Scripture and sacred Tradition, which is the living memory of the Church. God's covenants do not end, but come to greater fulfillment and realization.

The *Catechism of the Catholic Church* calls mission work "a requirement of the Church's catholicity" (see 848-849), meaning that because the Church is for all humanity, she must be a welcoming community that takes Christ's message to others. In fact, the Second Vatican Council called the Church "the universal sacrament of salvation" (*Lumen Gentium*, 48). We are the visible sign to the world that Christ welcomes all to life in him.

Taking Christ to the world is not only a collective responsibility, but also an individual one. In baptism, each follower of Christ is sent forth as missionary. In his encyclical letter *Redemptoris Missio*, Pope John Paul II wrote: "The mission *ad gentes* is incumbent upon the entire People of God. Whereas the foundation of a new church requires the Eucharist and hence the priestly ministry, missionary activity, which is carried out in a wide variety of ways, is the task of all the Christian faithful" (71). For this task, we draw upon sacred Tradition and, most especially, sacred Scripture: "And so the apostolic preaching, which is expressed in a special way in the inspired books, was to be preserved by an unending succession of preachers until the end of time" (*Dei Verbum*, 8).

The Church's Mission of Evangelization

In his apostolic exhortation on evangelization in the modern world (*Evangelii Nuntiandi*), Pope Paul VI outlines some essential elements of evangelization. These are restated in the *NDC* as "proclaiming Christ, preaching Christ, bearing witness to Christ, teaching Christ, and celebrating Christ's sacraments" (17). Pope Paul states that evangelization should result in the renewal of humanity and a change in how judgments are made and values are determined (*Evangelii Nuntiandi,* 19). He points to the witness of Christian lives as the most important element of evangelization, saying, "All Christians are called to this witness, and in this way they can be real evangelizers" (21).

Referencing Vatican II's *Decree on the Church's Missionary Activity (Ad Gentes)*, the *National Directory for Catechesis* discusses the "complex process of stages or moments" in evangelization (17):

1. **"Missionary activity directed toward non-believers or those who live in religious indifference":** This is the pre-evangelization stage, in which the listeners are prepared for the proclamation of the Gospel. This stage "builds on basic human needs, such as security, love, or acceptance, and shows how those basic human needs include a desire for God and his word."

2. **Initial proclamation of the Gospel (or "missionary preaching"):** In this stage, God's Word is presented to "children of Christians," as well as "non-believers, those who have chosen not to believe, [and] those who follow other religions." This type of evangelization is directed toward those who should be ready to hear the Gospel, but have not yet expressed any interest in its message.

3. **Initial catechetical activity for those who choose the Gospel or need to modify their initiation:** This stage includes catechesis for the sacraments of initiation, for children, youths, and adults who are coming to the Catholic faith, and those who are baptized but not fully initiated. This stage also includes mystagogical or post-baptismal catechesis, in which individuals learn how to live out the sacraments they have celebrated.

4. **Pastoral activity directed toward those of mature Christian faith:** Christians should continue to grow in the faith throughout their lives. This stage consists of the "permanent or continuing catechesis," or ongoing learning about the truths of the Christian faith and how they apply to everyday living.

The New Evangelization

In an address to catechists in 1999, Cardinal Joseph Ratzinger (later Pope Benedict XVI) said that to *evangelize* means "to teach the art of living ... to show the path." Evangelization is about more than what we say; it is about how we live, and who we follow. These are relevant issues, said Cardinal Ratzinger, for a time in which the de-Christianization of society has left so many people wondering how to live.

The developed or so-called First World countries — for example, countries in Europe and North America, which were evangelized long ago — have historically been leaders in science and technology, but the progress made in these areas in the last several generations has unfortunately not led to greater happiness. Additionally, in many Western societies, an increasing push to keep Christ out of the public square has made faith seem irrelevant to daily life.

All this has, according to Cardinal Ratzinger, led to a "deep poverty" — lives that are busy but without meaning — tedious routines, and an "inability to have joy." Jesus said, "I came so that they might have life and have it more abundantly" (Jn 10:10). God is waiting to fill us with meaning and hope. This is the purpose of the New Evangelization.

The New Evangelization is a call to each of us, to first renew our own faith and the experience of faith in our home, the domestic church. Then, we are called to take Christ's message to the world around us, which may "know about" Jesus but may not truly know Jesus until they hear our faith articulated and see it in action.

Essential Contents of the New Evangelization

Cardinal Ratzinger outlined the "essential contents" of the New Evangelization. The first and most basic message of the Christian faith is the mystery of the Holy Trinity. God is one God in three divine Persons. The Trinity lives in eternal mutual self-gift. God the Father has given himself completely to the Son. God the Son, in return, gives himself completely to the Father. The Spirit of love between the Father and the Son is so powerful, so tangible, that it literally becomes a third person — the Holy Spirit. This intimate communion, based on self-giving love, is a pattern for us as we follow Jesus' New Commandment to "love one another."

A second essential topic of the New Evangelization is the person of Jesus Christ. As Catholics we believe that Jesus, the Second Person of the Holy Trinity, became man — fully human and fully divine — in order to reveal to us the fullness of God's love and his plan for humankind. In a 2011 General Audience on the New Evangelization, Pope Benedict stated: "[Jesus'] death and resurrection are the Good News that, starting from Jerusalem, is destined to reach all people and nations, and to transform all cultures from within, opening them to the fundamental truth: God is love; he became man in Jesus, and with his sacrifice he ransomed humanity from slavery to evil, giving it a trustworthy hope." Relationship with the person of Jesus Christ is critical to the Christian life. We are called to *discipleship* — following Jesus and loving others as he did. Christ himself gives us a pattern for his way of life in the beatitudes.

Third, as much of Jesus' ministry involved proclaiming the kingdom of God, we are called to work with God as he builds his kingdom, and to share with others this invitation to God's kingdom. The kingdom of God, the reign of God's love and peace, exists now, and also is still to come. As we work toward peace, justice for all, and a world in which the poorest and most marginalized are cared for, we are working with God to build his kingdom. As we make God the center of our lives and call others to praise and honor him, we are working with God to build his kingdom. We look forward with hope to the time when we will live in the perfect and eternal reign of God when we are together with him in heaven.

Finally, a new evangelization celebrates the hope we have of eternal life. This eternal life — the "living water" that Jesus offers the woman at the well — is not only the home we have in heaven with God, but also the peace and meaning we have in this life when we respond to God's call and follow Jesus. Our ultimate destination is communion with God — to be one with him. We find real peace, ultimate happiness, and life eternal when we allow God's grace to form us into the people we were made to be.

Questions for Reflection

- What are some different ways to tell others about God?

- Who in my life has been the most powerful witness of Christ's love? Why?

Chapter 11

A SELF-PERPETUATING, EVANGELIZING CATECHESIS

OUR FAITH IS ROOTED IN MYSTERY, and should never be reduced to simplistic formulae or pat answers that fail to capture the imagination and fall short of conveying the depth and richness of God's revelation to humankind. For this reason, all catechesis should be permeated with the sense that, for each of us, there is still more to be understood about the great truths of the faith. This understanding will come gradually as disciples continue to reflect on the truth in the light of their own experiences and in the context of the whole of the Christian message. Catechists should encourage this process of continued study, reflection, and integration, which will ensure that the seeds of faith take root in the heart and continue to grow toward maturity.

Forms of the Message

There is one Gospel, but many forms of the message. The example we show others is just as important as what we say about

Christ, if not more so. Highlighting this point, Saint Francis of Assisi is often attributed with saying, "Preach the Gospel at all times ... when necessary, use words." We are called to tell others about Christ through the choices we make in our daily lives — the way we treat others, the priorities we set, and the way we do our work. "For all Christians, wherever they live, are bound to show forth, by the example of their lives and by the witness of the word, that new man put on at baptism and that power of the Holy Spirit by which they have been strengthened at Confirmation" (*Ad Gentes,* 11).

The environment in which we minister does not change the Gospel itself, but it may change the form of the message. The *General Directory of Catechesis* points out the necessity of presenting the Gospel message in its purity, but also states, "Evangelization will lose much of its power and efficacy if it does not take into consideration the people to whom it is addressed" (112). While we must hand on the authentic and complete message of Christ, we must be sensitive to individual and cultural needs.

In some cases, individuals, or even a society as a whole, are not ready to hear the Gospel message directly. In these cases, according to the Second Vatican Council, we can and ought to at least bear witness to the love and kindness of Christ, and thus "prepare the way for the Lord and make Him somehow present" (*Ad Gentes*, 6).

Catechesis and Evangelization

One particular challenge for catechists and catechetical leaders in the United States is that a particular group being catechized will often include individuals who are at various stages in the process of evangelization. Groups of children and teens especially may include those who need pre-evangelization because they are not open to the Gospel message. Others have never really heard or understood the Gospel. Still others may be preparing for the sacraments of initiation or working to more fully understand that which they have celebrated, and some individuals are in need of ongoing formation in the faith. It is important to know where people are if we are to communicate the Gospel in a way that they can can hear and respond. This realization challenges us to enter into the process of evangelization and catechesis with an attitude of openness to the Spirit and toward those whom we catechize.

Tools for the New Evangelization

The New Evangelization, according to Pope Benedict XVI, will mean acting locally, starting small, and surrendering to the "grain of the mustard seed." He cited this parable to remind us that God can do great things with small actions.

First, the foundation of prayer is essential. We must be open and receptive to the work of the Holy Spirit in our lives and in our culture. We must realize that as we listen for God's voice, we may be called to change the way in which we live.

As families and Christian communities, we are also called to continue growing in the way we follow Jesus' New Commandment to "love one another." Loving one another is not merely about loving our neighbor (for that was the "old commandment"). It is about cultivating *communion* — giving of ourselves and gratefully receiving the gift of others.

A New Evangelization will also involve using new forms of communication, such as social networking and other modern technologies, to spread the Gospel. Jesus is the same yesterday, today, and forever, but a missionary Church perpetually looks for ways to use modern innovations in the service of God.

Finally, a New Evangelization needs to tackle one of the oldest and deepest questions of human existence — the meaning of suffering. Our faith is unique in the redemptive meaning we assign to suffering, and there is much suffering in the world today. In an address to catechists on September 27, 2013, Pope Francis encouraged us not to be fearful as we encounter the suffering and the need of our human family, for as we go out, "God is always ahead of us! When we think about going far away, to an extreme outskirt, we may be a bit afraid, but in fact God is already there. Jesus is waiting for us in the hearts of our brothers and sisters, in their wounded bodies, in their hardships, in their lack of faith.

Empowered for the Mission

We are energized for our mission in the world by God's love for us (see 2 Cor 5:14; *Catechism of the Catholic Church*, 851). When we truly come to know God's love for us, we will naturally want to share that love with others.

The Holy Spirit, in particular, has a special role in historical and present-day mission work (*Ad Gentes*, 4). It was by the power of the Holy Spirit that Christ was conceived. The Spirit moved Christ to begin his ministry, and Christ sent the Spirit to the apostles at Pentecost, the birthday of the Church. The Holy Spirit continues to empower Christians today through the gifts of wisdom, understanding, counsel, fortitude, knowledge, piety, and fear of the Lord. Using the gifts of the Holy Spirit bears the fruits of "love, joy, peace, patience, kindness, generosity, faithfulness, gentleness, self-control" (Gal 5:22-23).

Our unity as believers should also be both a source of strength and witness to the faith we profess. Unfortunately, many divisions exist in the Church today, even among those who call themselves "Catholic," but especially within the Christian community as a whole. While ecumenical dialog is a distinctly different task from spreading the Gospel to those who have not yet heard it, the nature of our mission as Church calls us to work toward unity (*Catechism*, 855).

Those Who Are Not Catechized

Missionary activity is directed in a particular way toward those who do not know Christ or have never heard the basic Gospel message. In our more secular society, we are encountering more and more individuals in this situation. As Catholics, we believe in a just God who would provide a way of salvation for someone who had no opportunity to hear the Gospel. This does not, however, lessen our obligation to spread the Gospel message. God's will is that all should come to know him through his Church. Because, in God's design, since the Church is the *primary* vehicle for spreading the good news of Christ, we are called to work *as if* we were the only way others may come to know him, but we trust in God's mercy for those who do not come to know him through our efforts.

Therefore though God in ways known to himself can lead those inculpably ignorant of the Gospel to find that

faith without which it is impossible to please Him, yet a
necessity lies upon the Church, and at the same time a
sacred duty, to preach the Gospel. And hence missionary activity today as always retains its power and necessity. (*Ad Gentes*, 7)

It is up to each of us to plant and nurture the seeds of God's
Word in our world today and to point others to Christ. Jesus
calls his followers "the light of the world" and "the salt of the
earth" (Mt 5:13,14). Similarly, the Second Vatican Council
states that it is up to the laity "to be a leaven working on the
temporal order from within, to dispose it always in accordance
with Christ" (*Ad Gentes*, 15). We are called to change the world
from within by identifying the goodness and truth already present in humanity and relating these positive qualities to the God
who is their source. We are also charged with standing against
injustice and untruth in our world.

We can never know when or where the seed of God's word
may take root and grow, but this growth is God's work, not ours.
We bear witness to God's love and justice in hope that others
will respond, but in the end it is the witness of Christ in the
world that counts — celebrating God's love for us and giving
others a chance to know him.

Our catechesis can only mirror the self-perpetuating quality of the divine pedagogy if it is firmly rooted in a spirit of
mission. Missionary initiation is mentioned in the *General Directory for Catechesis* as one of the six fundamental tasks of catechesis (86). This task involves preparing individuals to spread
the Gospel to others by word and example. While only some
may be called to other lands to minister in Christ's name, *all* are
called to live in such a way that we serve as witnesses of the faith
to those who are around us. Catechists should work to instill an

understanding of evangelization as central to the mission of the Church and, by default, of every believer.

Catechists should prepare those being catechized to preach by example, and also articulate and defend their faith when called upon to do so. Saint Peter admonishes the believer to "always be ready to give an explanation to anyone who asks you for a reason for your hope" (1 Pt 3:15).

Finally, while all believers are called to mission in some way or another, catechists should encourage those being catechized, especially adults who are growing in their faith, to discern whether they might be called in some way to ministry of catechesis.

Questions for Reflection

- How does evangelization happen in your parish or school? What part do you play in this activity?

- How does your community reach out to those outside the community, including those not catechized and those of other religions?

Chapter 12

Resources for Catechetical Ministry

Scripture and Tradition

THE WORD OF GOD, as revealed in Scripture and sacred Tradition, is the primary source for catechesis (*National Directory for Catechesis*, 18). According to the *NDC*, it follows that catechesis is primarily based on the Old and New Testaments, interpreted in the context of the sacred deposit of faith. Use of Scripture in catechesis is emphasized in the *NDC*, particularly use of the Gospels to facilitate an "encounter with Christ." The Church provides guidance on the interpretation of Scripture:

- Take into account the time period, culture, and kind of writing (*Catechism*, 110).

- Read parts of Scripture in the context of the whole message (112).

- Read Scripture within "the living tradition of the whole Church" (113).

- Pay attention to the truths of faith expressed in Scripture. Great truths are always consistent with one another. For example, both the Old and New Testaments present love for God and love for one's neighbor as guiding principles of God's law.

In his book *The Parish Guide to the New Evangelization*, Fr. Robert Hater recommends several ways to extend biblically-based pastoral efforts in our parishes. His suggestions include the following:

- Opportunities for parishioners to study Scripture and pray with it in parish settings and in their homes.

- Love for and knowledge of Scripture on the part of the pastor and ministerial team.

- A resource center with Bibles, commentaries, books, and tapes about Scripture for borrow or purchase.

- Commitment to begin each parish project, meeting, or session with Scripture.

- Opportunities for children and youth catechists to learn the Scriptures.

- Sessions for parents, instructing them on how to teach Scripture to their children.

- Retreats and days of renewal based on Scripture.

- Catechetical sessions for children, youths, and adults, including children in Catholic schools, stressing the centrality of Scripture.

- A parish style that relates service functions to Scripture — for example, before a Saint Vincent de Paul meeting — where a participant reads a Scripture passage and discusses how Jesus' words and deeds relate to the group's ministerial activities.

- Homilies centered on applying Scripture to everyday life.

Catechisms

The *Catechism of the Catholic Church* presents a standard for catechesis. It is a summary of our sacred Tradition presented in the context of the contemporary world (*NDC*, 67). However, this universal catechism provides a more general overview and does not attempt to adapt catechesis to particular cultural situations and other special circumstances. This is the role of local catechisms. The *United States Catholic Catechism for Adults* is the local catechism for our country.

Catechetical Textbooks

Other resources for catechesis include textbooks, catechist guides, and supplemental materials. Texts are important because, when they are of high quality, they help to organize our catechetical approach and ensure the integrity of the message, assisting us in presenting a faithful, systematic, and comprehensive catechesis.

In choosing the textbook series that is most appropriate for a particular parish program, there are several aspects that should be considered. These can be organized most generally around the issues of content and methodology.

CONTENT

Perhaps the most important question with regard to content is, "Does this text present authentic Catholic teaching?" The word *catechesis* comes from the Greek word for "echo," implying that as catechists we echo the teachings of Christ and the apostles. The texts we use in a catechetical program must be theologically and doctrinally correct, so that we can truly say, with Jesus, "My teaching is not my own but is from the one who sent me." The U.S. Conference of Catholic Bishops has established a Subcommittee on the Catechism. A primary task of this committee is reviewing texts for children and youths, and evaluating them for theological content and doctrinal accuracy. The results of their reviews can be found on the USCCB website, where a current list is posted of texts found to be in conformity with the *Catechism*.

Another key issue related to content is the *Christocentricity* of the text. The *General Directory for Catechesis* states, "The definitive aim of catechesis is to put people not only in touch, but also in communion and intimacy, with Jesus Christ" (80). Christianity at its core is about discipleship, following, both individually and as a body, the person of Jesus Christ.

Finally, a good textbook series will be comprehensive in its approach. Every Catholic, and certainly every catechist, has aspects of the faith that they especially love — for example, devotion to the Blessed Mother, Catholic social teaching, Church history, or Catholic apologetics. These are all part of our rich and multifaceted faith. However, our task as catechists is not just to highlight those aspects of the faith for which we have a particular fondness. Rather, we are called to hand on the faith in its entirety. A textbook series, as an organizing tool for catechetical ministry, should present a comprehensive overview of the basic teachings of the Catholic faith. This is another important element assessed by the USCCB Subcommittee on the Catechism before texts are found to be in conformity. They must present the fullness of Catholic teaching.

Another useful framework for assessing the comprehensiveness of a textbook series is found in the *General Directory for Catechesis*. This document gives six "fundamental tasks of catechesis":

- **Promoting knowledge of the faith**: We cannot live a faith we do not know. For this reason, studying the teachings of Jesus and his Church is an essential task of catechesis.

- **Liturgical education**: This task relates to learning about the ways in which the Church worships and celebrates, including the seven sacraments, the Order of Mass, and the liturgical year.

- **Moral formation**: This task of catechesis involves forming the consciences of learners through the moral teachings of Jesus and his Church, and fostering understanding of what it means to live these teachings in one's daily life.

- **Teaching to pray**: This task of catechesis involves teaching the traditional prayers of the Church, and the various forms and expressions of prayer. It involves fostering an understanding of prayer as conversation with God — teaching how to talk with God in one's own words as well as how to listen to God.

- **Education for community life**: This task of catechesis relates to developing an understanding of what it means to be a part of the Christian community, including respecting the authority and structure of the Church as well as living out Jesus' New Commandment to love one another as he has loved us.

- **Missionary initiation**: All Christians are called, by virtue of their baptism, to be witnesses of Jesus Christ in both word and deed. This task of catechesis prepares the learner to share his or her faith with others.

A comprehensive textbook series will provide tools for catechists to engage in each of these fundamental tasks with their learners in developmentally appropriate ways.

METHODOLOGY

The *General Directory for Catechesis* points out that **a variety of methodologies are appropriate for use in catechesis,** stating that "perfect fidelity to Catholic doctrine is compatible with a rich diversity of presentation" (122). In fact, the *GDC* goes on to say that "the 'variety of methods is a sign of life and richness' as well as a demonstration of respect for those to whom catechesis is addressed" (148). Using methods that are appropriate to the particular learner, group, or environment help to engage the learner, to show that our message is both living and rich. We also show respect for the learner by tailoring our message to his or her needs.

Multiple methods are important when we consider what educational research tells us about how people of various ages learn best. Children and teens especially are most likely to pay attention to information, and to remember it, when it is presented in a variety of forms. Therefore, a good textbook series should provide a variety of visual, auditory, and kinesthetic activities to reinforce key teachings. It should also present teachings systematically such that key definitions and concepts are presented as a child or teen is developmentally able to understand them. What a shame it would be to have an authentic message delivered in a form in which children were unlikely to fully understand, pay attention, or remember! A good catechetical series will involve professionals trained in education and child development as well as theology in creating the materials to ensure that the message is presented in a way that children and teens can hear and understand, as well as in a way that reflects what the Church teaches.

Another important aspect of methodology relates to the catechist. **A good textbook series should have catechist manuals that are understandable and easy to use.** It should include material that assists in the catechist formation and reflection, since we cannot hand on a faith that we ourselves do not know or practice.

Finally, remembering the Church teaching that parents are the first and most important catechists of their children, **a catechetical textbook series should provide resources for parents and families to talk about and practice their faith at**

home. The parish is called to assist families by articulating and organizing the key teachings of the Church, which should be lived out at home as the ultimate witness of what Catholics believe and practice.

Content and methodology are not, as some would have us believe, opposite poles of the same continuum. It is not the case that parishes must choose between a curriculum that is doctrinally correct, or one that is developmentally appropriate. Both content and methodology are essential to faithful and effective transmission of our Catholic faith to the next generation.

To summarize, here are some questions to ask when choosing a catechetical text:

- Does the series present an authentic and comprehensive overview of the Church teaching?

- Has the USCCB Ad Hoc Committee to Oversee the Use of the Catechism found the series to be in conformity with the *Catechism of the Catholic Church*?

- Does the series foster knowledge of, and relationship with, the person of Jesus Church and his body, the Church?

- Does the series give due attention to each of the six fundamental tasks of catechesis outlined in the *General Directory for Catechesis*?

- Does the textbook employ a variety of learning methodologies, appropriate to children and teens of various ages and abilities?

- Are adaptations provided to assist learners with disabilities?

- Are the catechist manuals straightforward and easy to use? Do they provide some formation and personal reflection to help foster the catechist's own faith development?

- Are practical tools given to help involve parents and families and assist them in living their faith at home?

Chapter 10 in the *National Directory for Catechesis* lists several guidelines for the selection of catechetical textbooks. The *NDC* also points out that merely translating catechetical texts is often not enough to facilitate a bilingual program or provide catechesis to persons who speak other languages. When possible, catechetical textbooks in other languages should be written by native speakers of those languages, who understand the nuances of the language and cultural factors that may impact communication.

The Importance of the Catechist as a Resource for Catechetical Ministry

While selection of textbooks and other resources is important, it should also be remembered that formation is, first and foremost, an apprenticeship in the Christian life. Individuals being formed in the faith learn best by living out their faith and interacting with individuals who are good examples of Christian living. The *General Directory for Catechesis* emphasizes the importance of the catechist in this process:

No methodology, no matter how well tested, can dispense with the person of the catechist in every phase of the catechetical process. The charism given to him by the Spirit, a solid spirituality and transparent witness of life, constitutes the soul of every method. Only his own human and Christian qualities guarantee a good use of texts and other work instruments. (156)

Because the person of the catechist is so essential to catechetical ministry, the next chapter will focus on the selection and formation of catechists.

Questions for Reflection

- How do I use sacred Scripture and sacred Tradition in my work as a catechist?

- Which of the six tasks of catechesis do our current resources cover well? For which tasks of catechesis might I need to find additional resources?

Chapter 13

The Pedagogy of God and the Selection and Formation of Catechists

The understanding of the divine pedagogy as the pattern for catechesis also has implications for the selection and formation of catechists. Catechesis is an essential ministry of the Church, and those called to catechesis have been given a charism from the Holy Spirit to do this work (*NDC*, 54.B.8). Because of this, catechetical leaders should take special care in how they recruit individuals to serve in this ministry. The *National Directory for Catechists* strongly cautions against implying that "anyone can be a catechist" (55.B). The *Guide for Catechists*, by the Vatican's Congregation for the Evangelization of Peoples, lists several characteristics that should be observed in those who will serve as catechists. This list is cited in the *NDC*:

Faith that manifests itself in their piety and daily life; love for the Church and communion with its pastors; apostolic spirit and missionary zeal; love for their brothers and sisters and a willingness to give generous service; sufficient education; the respect of the community; the human, moral and technical qualities necessary for the work of a catechist, such as dynamism, good relations with others, etc." (*Guide for Catechists*, 18)

The *NDC* adds that a catechist should rise from within the parish community and be invited by the pastor in consultation with the parish catechetical leader.

The *General Directory for Catechesis* (237) offers criteria for the formation of catechists:

- Catechists should be formed "to evangelize in the present historical context, with its values, challenges, and disappointments."

- Formation should take into account "the *concept of catechesis*, proposed by the Church today.... Catechists must be able to be, at one and the same time, teachers, educators, and witnesses of the faith."

- Catechists must be able to integrate multiple facets of the catechetical process — "the dimension of truth and meaning of the faith, orthodoxy and orthopraxis, ecclesial and social meaning."

- Formation should take into account "the *specific character of the laity in the Church*" and not treat the work and mission of catechists as simply an extension of the work of priests and religious.

And perhaps most relevant to the present discussion:

- The pedagogy used in catechetical formation should be analogous to the "pedagogy proper to the catechetical process." In other words, it should also be based on the pedagogy of God. As the *GDC* points out, "It would be very difficult for the catechist in his activity to improvise a style and sensibility to which he had not been introduced during his own formation" (237).

According to the *NDC*, initial formation of catechists should: help them understand "the social, cultural, ethnic, demographic, and religious circumstances of the people [the catechist] will serve"; be respectful of their time constraints while still providing a structured and systematic overview of the ministry; develop their human, spiritual, and apostolic qualities; facilitate the catechist's prayer life and communication with the local church; encourage new catechists to connect with others in the ministry, perhaps even forming mentoring relationships; encourage catechists to seek out a spiritual director; and "remain within the context of the community of faith" (55.D).

Ongoing formation is also necessary, as it is for all Christians. For catechists especially, this means ongoing development of human qualities (emotional growth, communication skills, etc.) as well as growth in spirituality and knowledge of the faith. Catechetical methodology and social science — for example, psychology, education, and communication — are also topics for continued study by catechists.

A variety of settings exist for catechist formation, and each has its own benefits. Parish-based formation, diocesan events, retreats, seminars and training, and classes sponsored by Catholic universities can all be beneficial in different ways. For example, formation in the parish setting helps catechists working together to get to know one another and can be useful for discussing issues that are particular to a given parish, while diocesan and regional events can help catechists appreciate their own work within the context of the catechetical mission of the Church worldwide.

Questions for Reflection

- How was I called to the ministry of catechesis?

- What processes are currently available for formation of catechists in my parish? In what areas is stronger formation needed?

Church Documents Cited
in *The Way God Teaches*

Congregation for the Clergy. *General Directory for Catechesis*, 1997.

Congregation for the Evangelization of Peoples. *Guide for Catechists*. Document of vocational, formative and promotional orientation of catechists in the territories dependent on the Congregation for the Evangelization of Peoples, 1993.

Interdicasterial Commission for the *Catechism of the Catholic Church*. *Catechism of the Catholic Church*, 1992.

John Paul II. Apostolic exhortation *Catechesi Tradendae*, 1979.

———. Post-synodal apostolic exhortation *Familiaris Consortio*, 1981.

———. Encyclical letter *Redemptoris Missio*, 1991.

———. Apostolic exhortation *Novo Millenio Inuente*, 2000.

Pontifical Council for the Family. *The Truth and Meaning of Human Sexuality: Guidelines for Education Within the Family*, 1995.

Sacred Congregation for the Clergy. *General Catechetical Directory*, 1972.

Second Vatican Council. Dogmatic Constitution on the Church, *Lumen Gentium*, 1964.

———. Dogmatic Constitution on Divine Revelation, *Dei Verbum*, 1965.

———. Pastoral Constitution on the Church in the Modern World, *Gaudium et Spes*, 1965.

United States Catholic Conference. *Sharing the Light of Faith: The National Catechetical Directory for Catholics of the United States* (1979 *National Directory*). Washington, D.C.: United States Catholic Conference, 1979.

———. *Human Sexuality: A Catholic Perspective for Education and Lifelong Learning*. Washington, D.C.: United States Catholic Conference, 1991.

———. *Welcome and Justice for Persons with Disabilities: A Framework of Access and Inclusion*. Washington, D.C.: United States Catholic Conference, 1998.

———. *National Directory for Catechesis*. Washington, D.C.: USCCB Publishing, 2005.

Additional Works Cited

Augustine of Hippo. *Sermo 227*, in *Sermons, Volume III/6 184-299*. Hyde Park, NY: New City Press, 1993.

Bonhoeffer, Dietrich. *The Cost of Discipleship*. New York: Macmillan Publishing Corp., 1963.

Dilorio, Colleen, Kelley, Maureen, and Hockenberry-Eaton, Marilyn (1999). "Communications about Sexual Issues: Mothers, Fathers, and Friends." Journal of Adolescent Health, 24(3) (1999): 181-189.

Gardner, Howard. *Frames of Mind: The Theory of Multiple Intelligences*. New York: Basic Books, 1983.

Jaccard, James, Dittus, Patricia, and Gordon, Vivian. "Parent-Teen Communication about Premarital Sex: Factors Associated with the Extent of Communication." Journal of Adolescent Research, 15(2) (2000): 187-208.

Karofsky, Peter S., Zeng, Lan, and Kosorok, Michael R. "Relationship Between Adolescent-Parental Communication and Initiation of First Intercourse by Adolescents." Journal of Adolescent Health, 28(1) (2000): 41-45.

Lederman, Regina P., Chan, Wenyaw, and Roberts-Gray, Cynthia. "Sexual Risk Attitudes and Intentions of Youth Aged 12-14 Years; Survey Comparisons of Parent-Teen Prevention and Control Groups." Behavioral Medicine, 29(4) (2004): 155-163.

Neisser, Ulric. *Cognitive Psychology.* New York: Appleton-Century-Crofts, 1967.

Resnick, Michael, Bearman, Peter, Blum, Robert, et al. "Protecting Adolescents from Harm. Findings from the National Longitudinal Study on Adolescent Health." Journal of the American Medical Association, 278(10) (1997): 823-832.

Whitaker, Daniel, and Miller, Kim. "Parent-Adolescent Discussions about Sex and Condoms: Impact on Peer Influences of Sexual Risk Behavior." Journal of Adolescent Research, 15(2) (2000): 251-273.

Willey, Petroc. *Introductory Paper,* Catechetical Conference on the Pedagogy of God, Rome, Italy, 2009.